VERMONT
A View from Above

The name Vermont comes from the French for green mountains, the dominant geological feature in the state. The Green Mountain range extends right through Vermont from south to north, splitting the difference between the Connecticut river on the east and lake Champlain on the west. This photograph, taken at mid-morning south of Fair Haven, combines the elements of water, mountains, and a farmstead tucked into a valley.

VERMONT
A View from Above

CHARLES FEIL

With notes by Tom Slayton, *Vermont Life* Magazine

Down East Books   Camden, Maine

Copyright © 1999 by Charles William Feil III
ISBN 0-89272-458-7
Book design by Janet Patterson
Color separations, printing, and binding by Oceanic Graphic Printing
Printed in China

3   5   4   2

Down East Books/Camden, Maine

LIBRARY OF CONGRESS CATALOGING-IN-PUBLICATION DATA

Feil, Charles, 1948–
       Vermont, a view from above / Charles Feil.
           p.   cm.
       ISBN 0-89272-458-7 (hardcover)
       1. Vermont—Aerial photographs. I. Title.
   F50 .F45 1999
   917.43'0022'2—dc21   98-33131
                                                        CIP

Acknowledgments

To Maralyce Ferree for all her loving support while I was on the road.

To my son, Dylan, for his sensitive insights.

Byron Danforth, for making his home, my home, and allowing me to utilize the facilities at Middlebury State Airport—where "hangar chat" became a major source of information for this book.

Leo Dewey Jr. and Nancy Fratti, who came to my salvation in Fairhaven when I needed a bath and a good meal.

To all the general aviation pilots, who will truly appreciate what these photographs are about.

To the air traffic controllers—especially in Burlington, Vermont—who have been my eyes in the sky all these years.

A special thanks to Tom Slayton of Vermont Life for his introductions to the regions and the accuracy of my captions.

Janet Patterson for taking my photographs and harmonizing them into a beautiful design.

Last, but not least, the great staff at Down East Books—Neal Sweet, Karin Womer, Chris Cornell, and Terry Bregy, who have believed in and supported this unique concept from the beginning.

— C. F.

The Middlebury community describes itself this way: "Our heart is Middlebury, Shire Town of Addison County. Our playground stretches from Rutland to Burlington, from the Green Mountains to beautiful Lake Champlain." The town's airport provided me with a home base for a major part of this book, so much of my affection for Vermont took seed in Middlebury.

Dusk had turned to twilight

as I switched off the lights in my Scarborough, Maine, studio and headed out to my pickup. The truck was already sitting low on the asphalt under its burden of a camper unit and a trailer loaded with my marvelous flying machine—a gyroplane I call *Rooty Kazooty.*

We lumbered out of the driveway and headed south on I-95 toward the New Hampshire border, then west on Route 4 to the Vermont line. It was one of those perfect, full-moon New England summer evenings that you like to hold in your memory for the cold winter season. I was beginning a marvelous adventure—to begin photographing the Green Mountain State from above. This was not just another attempt to snap some quaint village bathed in early-morning sunlight, but an effort to capture the moods, textures, and capricious nature of the Vermont landscape from the air—just as I had done in Maine and Massachusetts.

The next day, I hadn't yet made a decision about where to start, so I decided to let my intuition pick a spot. I dug out a map and chose the Rutland area, but changed my mind after meeting a gentleman who told me about a small airstrip west of Rutland, in the town of Fair Haven, right on the border between Vermont and New York. He offered to show me its location, and I followed him over the hills and through the valleys to my first base of operations. This was a *Rooty Kazooty* heaven, with an old rundown wooden hangar and a two-thousand-foot gravel runway shared by model-airplane enthusiasts and ATV riders, as well as a couple of well flown Piper Cubs.

I would fit into this mix nicely and be relatively undisturbed—or so I thought. My arrival just happened to coincide with the appearance of a group of Shriners who were setting up an annual gathering marked by drink, food, and bravado. A half-dozen of these jovial gents wandered over to see what I was hauling out of my trailer. It wasn't long before "hangar talk" began to surface, and there were plenty of willing hands to help me attach *Rooty Kazooty*'s rotor blades. I knew my audience was anxious to see this little bug fly, so with a good deal of fanfare, *Rooty* and I took to the skies for a little solitude and a demonstration of the gyroplane's agility.

Rooty Kazooty

After I had landed and secured *Rooty* for the night, one of the Shriners came over and invited me to join in the festivities. I answered the usual barrage of questions as I devoured a Maine lobster and a couple of cold beers. Toward the end of the party I engaged in a conversation with Leo, an intense thinker who likes to delve into the mystical and magical qualities of the universe. As our conversation continued into the late afternoon, Leo began to portray me as a kind of Donald Shimoda, a mythical barnstorming guru in Richard Bach's book *Illusions*. I was flattered by the comparison, but I managed to keep my ego in check.

Over the next several days, Leo would show up at my camper and offer to take me out to buy food and fuel, eager to peel back more layers of the mind. As a thank-you for all his help and friendship I invited him for a flight in *Rooty Kazooty*. He lit up like a Christmas tree as we soared over the hills, valleys, and lakes of central Vermont.

As it turned out, Leo, his fellow Shriners, and the gentleman who showed me the airstrip in Fair Haven were just the first of many fine people who would, in one way or another, contribute to this book. I was still in my first week of flying around the Vermont countryside, when I stumbled onto the next character in my adventure.

It was early on a Saturday morning when I lifted off from Fair Haven in a sea of mist and filtered sunshine to photograph the moods of Lake Champlain and the soothing textures of farmland in the Champlain Valley. Around mid-morning I was in need of a fuel stop and chose the airport in nearby Middlebury, which is nestled on the western fringes of the Green Mountains, about thirty miles south of Burlington. I swooped down and made a spot landing in front of an old wooden hangar.

Almost immediately, a husky man of about fifty—with the name BYRON embroidered on his blue shirt—ran out and greeted me with such excitement that I half-believed Leo's earlier assessment of my knack for being in the right place at the right time. Apparently, Byron had been talking about gyroplanes just the day before with a group of local aviation enthusiasts.

The usual conversation ensued, and I was invited in for coffee after refueling *Rooty*'s hungry tank. As soon as I set foot in the FBO (Flight Base Operations), I knew this was home to the local pilot population. A big wooden table was littered with an assortment of aviation magazines, and a large chart of the flying environment of the United States was tacked to the wall. This was the domain of Byron Danforth, an endangered species in our slowly eroding grassroots aviation community.

At the airport in Middlebury, he is chief mechanic, flight-school instructor, and paper pusher; in fact, he lives in a bungalow adjacent to the FBO. It is his kind of energy and enthusiasm that is helping to keep general aviation alive in this age of corporate mergers, when bigger operations find it unprofitable and even undesirable to tolerate neophytes who hang around, listening to and learning from veterans of the air.

For some days, I had been ready to move my base of operation farther north than Fair Haven, so I asked Byron if I might be able to set up camp at his airport. He agreed, and thus began a long, rewarding friendship built on mutual respect, favorite recipes, "wrenching" (working on airplane engines), and late-night stories from our mental closets. It was just such warm, relaxing experiences on the ground that helped me to focus my skills each day in the skies above the Green Mountain State.

It is now my privilege to share with you some of my photographic experiences above Vermont and my pleasure to thank all of the appealing people who welcomed me into their hearts and minds. This book is dedicated to you. Enjoy the view!

Charles Feil
Portland, Maine
February 1999

A view of Vermont from the

air does something no politician has ever been able to accomplish: it unifies the state, and shows how many similarities the different regions of Vermont share. From a thousand feet up, one white-spired church looks pretty much like another, a river is a river, and the valley it defines looks a lot like the valley over the next line of hills. The smaller concerns of everyday life fade when viewed from far above, and even mountains lose some of their hulking individuality, changing into carpeted textures of rock and forest.

What emerges, when viewed from above, are the unseen, universal patterns of the landscape. Chuck Feil has a superlative eye for such patterns, and they make his aerial photographs unusual and compelling.

Yet we should look at these fine photographs attentively; there's a hidden truth here. While at first it seems that the same mix of farmland, forest, villages, and winding river valleys carpets all of Vermont, there are subtle differences in each part of the state. A Vermonter blindfolded, spirited away, and released in downtown Dorset would know in an instant he was a long way from the Northeast Kingdom or the Champlain Valley. Likewise, Middlebury doesn't feel much like Northfield, even though both are college towns of similar size. Vermont is actually a state of subtle but distinct regions — not one landscape, but many. It is the broad vistas of the Champlain Valley and the historic villages of southern Vermont; the exciting cityscape of Burlington and the quiet rural farmscapes of the Northeast Kingdom. It is mountains and pastures, forests and lake shore. It is all these and more.

And because it has a varied landscape, Vermont is a visual feast all through the year for tourists, hikers, photographers, visitors of all sorts, and those of us lucky enough to live here. The seasons add their own variations to the mix. The result is that there's always something new to see and think about in this very old landscape.

Tom Slayton, Editor-in-Chief
Vermont Life Magazine
Montpelier, Vermont

Between Brattleboro and Bennington, Route 9 snakes its way through hills whose foliage is just beginning to show the colors of fall.

Isle La Motte is the northwesternmost of Lake Champlain's large islands. From above, you can witness the blend of lake water and sun that is ideal for the raising of crops and livestock on the farms bordering Blanchard Bay.

The Champlain Valley

Most of central Vermont lies wrapped in mountains, and the Green Mountain chain dominates the central part of the state. But the history of the place we know today as Vermont actually began in a valley—the Champlain Valley, wherein lies that stunningly beautiful expanse of fresh water that Samuel de Champlain discovered and named, with little modesty but unerring good sense, for himself. Even though our name is French, we often forget that Vermont was discovered by the French, from the north, via Lake Champlain. For roughly a century, the lake and the broad, beautiful valley that contains it marked the course of empire as first the French, then the British, and finally the colonial settlers who became Americans struggled for control of the strategic waterway that led from Canada through the heart of the colonies directly to the Hudson Valley and New York.

Today the Champlain Valley is home to more than a quarter of Vermont's population. It boasts some of the best farmland in New England, and is one of the few places in the region where broad, sweeping pastoral views dominate the landscape. The state's largest city—some say its only true city, Burlington—is the hub of the region, which also contains thousands of acres of productive farmland and a freshwater maritime heritage with a distinctive Vermont stamp.

—T. S.

Sheep farming in Vermont dates back to the 18th century, when the state's earliest settlers brought the animals along as part of their family farming operations. I photographed these sheep as I soared over Savage Island on Lake Champlain, between Grand Isle and the mainland.

A small summer cottage sits perched on the forested cliff of Butler Island, located between North Hero Island, in Lake Champlain, and St. Albans, on the mainland. Flying above Vermont is a wonderful way of discovering these secluded hideaways.

Breakwaters often play dual roles. One is to create a protective harbor for boats, and the other is to provide a crossing, which was the purpose of this breakwater between North Hero and Grand Isle on Lake Champlain.

Vacant in late fall, a campground at North Hero State Park on Lake Champlain awaits next summer's tourists. The park is popular for its size, relatively undisturbed condition, and rare flora.

Burlington is the largest city in Vermont and has the reputation of being an enlightened place to live, play, work, and visit. This is also the home of a variety of innovative companies such as Ben & Jerry's Ice Cream, Burton snowboards, and IDX medical software.

Vermont supplies a lot of solid and crushed rock to the rest of the world. This gravel pit, on the outskirts of Burlington, is one of many scattered throughout the state.

Located in Burlington, the University of Vermont was chartered in 1791, the same year that Vermont became the fourteenth state in the union. It was the first American institution of higher learning to declare that the "rules, regulations, and by-laws shall not tend to give preference to any religious sect or denomination whatsoever."

I do find it a bit incongruous to see the grand old steamer *Ticonderoga* several miles inland, in the town of Shelburne, instead of plying the waters it served for so many decades. Declared a National Historic Landmark in 1960, the vessel is America's last remaining side paddlewheel passenger steamer with a vertical beam engine.

One of the main attractions at the Shelburne Museum is the Round Barn, a three-story building that measures eighty feet in diameter. Originally constructed in 1901 by Fred "Silo" Quimby in East Passumpsic, Vermont, it was moved to Shelburne in 1986. Designed to increase the dairy farmer's efficiency, round barns were popular throughout New England in the late 19th and early 20th centuries.

The former estate of Dr. and Mrs. William Steward Webb, just a stone's throw south of Burlington, hosts the Vermont Symphony during the summer festival season. A railroad entrepreneur, Dr. Webb began amassing the 4,000-acre Shelburne Farms in the late 1800s. Now owned by a nonprofit corporation, it was known as one of the grandest estates in New England and the premier one in Vermont.

On a quiet summer's evening along the shores of Lake Champlain, I flew over this quaint homestead on Quaker Smith Point, just west of Shelburne, bathed in the glow of the setting sun.

Vergennes has an interesting and important place in Vermont history. It is the third oldest incorporated city in the United States and is reputed to be the smallest city in the country. From the air, you clearly see the relics of industrial and commercial enterprises that once prospered near Otter Creek Falls.

A Lake Champlain ferry navigates between moored sailboats in McNeil Cove. The ferries provide a relaxing and convenient way for commuters and travelers to shorten their trips between New York State and Vermont. This vessel transports its passengers and related cargo between Charlotte, Vermont, and Essex, New York.

Riding a stiff breeze out of the northwest, this yachtsman might be sailing on a much larger body of water than Lake Champlain.

Winterized sailboats await the wrath of winter weather at Thompson's Point Marina on the shores of Lake Champlain's Town Farm Bay.

Aglow in the early morning sun, the Crown Point bridge connects Chimney Point, Vermont, with Crown Point, New York. The mountains in the distance are the famed Adirondacks.

The turboprop cropduster is one of the modern tools that some farmers in Addison County and nearby Weybridge use cooperatively to combat crop disease and insects.

In late fall, migrating Canada geese and snow geese flock to the freshly harvested fields along Dead Creek, west of the town of Addison. The area is an ideal stopover on the birds' long journey south.

The year I photographed Vermont from above, winter started off more like spring. This allowed me to capture the leafless landscape *sans* snow. Late-afternoon winter light is remarkable for its deep rich tones, seen here carpeting the rolling countryside of a dairy farm near Weybridge.

Middlebury College began from humble roots in November 1800, when a number of Middlebury citizens took on the challenge of building an institution of higher learning on the American frontier. Two centuries later, "the town's college" has developed an international reputation for its academic excellence.

Shard Villa, in West Salisbury, is another example of the numerous Victorian mansions to be found throughout Vermont. From above, I was struck by its forbidding appearance in the middle of countryside more noted for its modest homesteads.

Each of my previous aerial-photography books has included a shot of an auto salvage yard. So, Vermont, this is your portrait of a great transportation recycling center: Blaise's Salvage yard, along Route 7 outside East Middlebury.

The meandering Lemon Fair River, near Sudbury, feeds nearby farmland, helping to keep the Champlain Valley a fertile area in which to raise crops, livestock, or a family.

Flying low over this tree, standing as a sentinel over a freshly harvested field north of Benson, was a joy not to be missed by the photographer or the pilot in me.

An abandoned covered bridge mirrors its modern counterpart where Route 73 crosses Otter Creek west of Brandon. At the turn of the century, road builders correctly concluded that a roof both protected open bridges from severe weather and added structural strength. Moreover, the enclosed sides shielded farm animals from frightening views.

This old rural church near Orwell seemed untouchable, as if the ring of trees were protecting the building from the world around it.

Sometimes the universe conspires to bring everything together for an airborne photographer. On the outskirts of Shoreham, this convergence of white cows and a lone black bull was truly serendipitous.

Fair Haven is a quiet village on the western edge of Vermont. A little-used gravel airstrip on the outskirts of town was my first home base in the state.

Early winter reveals the numerous cabins hidden behind the trees of Cones Point, along the shores of Lake St. Catherine, in Wells.

Southwestern Vermont

South of Lake Champlain, two smaller valleys meet in the shadow of the Taconic Mountains — a smaller range that parallels the southern Green Mountains a few miles to the west. The Valley of Vermont runs north-south, dividing the two ranges, and at Manchester the Mettowee Valley angles off the main valley to the northwest, bisecting the Taconic Range near Dorset. This southwestern area of Vermont is a region of rolling farmland, small villages, mountain recreation, and resorts.

Anchored by Bennington to the south, it is also a place rich in history, for it is here, in Bennington and Arlington, that Ethan Allen first gathered his Green Mountain Boys and began the legendary struggle that would one day make Vermont an independent republic and later a state.

— T. S.

Between Manchester Center and Bennington, the Valley of Vermont separates the Green Mountains to the east and the Taconic Mountains to the west. Route 7A is the old road that runs down this valley and through quaint villages like Arlington.

Green Mountain College, in Poultney, describes itself as "an environmental liberal arts college with an international focus that appeals to a rugged individualist who is an active learner looking for a shared community. Bring your boots!"

The owner of this farm, near Pawlet, seems to prefer fencing his hay rather than his livestock.

The alchemy of a good photograph is part luck and part technique. This rainbow suddenly appeared in my lens as I was circling golfers at the Ekwanok Country Club, in Manchester.

The Old Depot School in Shaftsbury is a one-room, four-grade schoolhouse that operated into the late 1950s.
My friend and fellow pilot Byron Danforth of Middlebury Flight School told me about his old alma mater,
and I found it by following a map he had drawn on the back of a napkin.

A cultivated field outside Middletown Spring reveals itself as artwork, transcending the mere labor of a farmer's tractor.

Skeletal trees haunt a watery graveyard at Lake Shaftsbury State Park.

Headstones and roadways converge in a cemetery south of Bennington.

On a dirt road behind the historic Park McCullough House in North Bennington, two hikers make their way to the beckoning hills. I banked Rooty hard to the left, grabbed my camera off the seat, and quickly composed this photo.

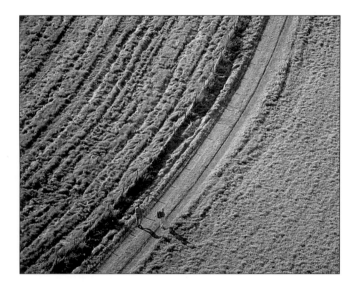

I made this photograph just before Halloween, when an enterprising farmer outside of Bennington turned a field of wilted stalks of corn into a diabolical maze.

Photographed here on a quiet Sunday morning, Bennington College sees itself as a place to learn, not merely as another career institution.

One of historic Bennington's downtown streets shows off its mixture of residential and commercial buildings.

Stoically sitting atop a hill on the western fringes of Bennington, this battle monument was erected in 1891 to commemorate the location of the Colonial stores over which the Battle of Bennington was fought.

As Rooty and I flew over a mountain ridge, a sliver of sunlight broke through a cloud and highlighted this farmstead in the Mettowee Valley.

Winter recreation is big business in Vermont, and the long list of ski areas includes the sprawling mountain known as Okemo. Below, in the valley, the village of Ludlow comes alive as it hosts nightlife highlighted by the outlandish ski stories of the day.

The Central Highlands

We are the Green Mountain State, to be sure, and the long, bumpy spine of mountains that curves roughly down the middle of the state has shaped Vermont culturally as well as physically. Until recently the spoken accents of native Vermonters were subtly different on the west and east sides of the mountains, and a century ago, the unwritten "mountain rule" of Vermont politics dictated that Vermont's governor would come from the west side one term, the east side the next. That was a way of making sure that all of Vermont got fair State House representation in the days when getting across the mountains was no small thing.

Those days are gone, but the mountains still play an important role in the everyday life of Vermont. Many of them now have ski areas on their flanks, and their forests yield sawlogs and paper pulp, framing timber and fine furniture. More than that, the mountains are also companions to the farms and villages at their feet. They are where Vermonters go to hunt and hike and ski, and where some Vermonters live. They are familiar landmarks, everyday presences for their human neighbors.

Montpelier, the state capital, is located in the heart of the mountains, near the geographic center of the state, and is emblematic of the state as a whole. It is the smallest state capital in the nation, and deer sometimes graze the lawn of the elegant little state house, backed by the surrounding wooded hills.

—T. S.

Named after Viscount Ludlow, this village sits at the base of what once was called Ludlow Mountain, which is now called Okemo Mountain due to the growth of the local ski area by that name.

These experimental wind-power generators off Route 9, near Wilmington, are an example of Vermont's forward-thinking approach to energy conservation.

A tractor harvests newly cut hay from a field south of Rutland.

Flying through the valleys along the western slopes of the Green Mountains, I came across this church gathering in a little community near Rutland.

The seven mountains of the Killington resort are in the heart of Vermont's ski country. Comprising some ninety-five miles of skiing and snowboarding terrain, this is one of the largest winter-recreation facilities in the world. When the snows melt, many of the trails are used for biking and hiking.

Scenic Route 100 is the main artery running through ski country and is fondly known as the "Ski Highway." Here, the road passes through the village of Waitsfield, in the Mad River valley.

Route 7 snakes its way from Burlington to Bennington, and along its path lie many quaint towns and villages worth a stopover. Pittsford is one of those that deserves a closer look.

A slice of late-afternoon sunlight reflects off the branches of a fresh snowfall in the Stockbridge area of the Green Mountain National Forest.

Vermont's wealth of slate, marble, and granite was discovered by the state's first settlers. This winter-shrouded quarry, near Bethel, seems literally frozen in time.

A fresh snowfall on a cold January afternoon provides skiers at the Sugarbush Resort in Warren with yet another challenge on its extensive network of already exciting trails.

Silver Lake sits atop the western slopes of the Green Mountains, south of Middlebury. Its sister, Lake Dunmore, straddles the hillside below. Together they represent a legacy of geological history—the great Ice Age that sculpted Vermont's mountains and carved out the lakes of her central highlands.

My mind's eye is always playing with the juxtaposition of shapes, forms, and textures I see from above, as in this wintry mix of branches and trees in the Chelsea area.

Heading east from Montpelier on Route 62, I came across the city of Barre, which is known as the Granite Capital of the world. A number of granite sculptures in the downtown area celebrate this reputation.

Snowmobiling is a very popular winter sport in Vermont. Here, a group of riders pauses for a break along a trail in the North Fayston area.

Sitting just below a snow-covered hillside in a picturesque valley along the Winooski River is Vermont's capital city, Montpelier. A gold-leaf dome proudly proclaims the capitol's distinction as our nation's smallest. Good things *do* come in small packages.

Looking more like a game of pick-up sticks, these aged trees in a bog near Marshfield have finally succumbed to the elements and await their transition back into the soil from which they came.

Winter strips the green skin from Camel's Hump west of Waterbury, revealing a skeleton of steep ravines and undulating bulges, with a prickly spine of sturdy hardwood trees.

In the still winds of an early fall morning, the "Stoweflake" balloon quietly glides over the pastoral valleys and rugged mountains of the Stowe area, giving its passengers a hawk's-eye view of the deciduous trees in all their glory.

Under a fresh snowfall, the fairy-tale village of Stowe beckons skiers and winter enthusiasts from all over New England and the rest of the country.

Fall colors outline the ski trails on Mount Mansfield, Vermont's highest peak. They await the winter season's first snowfall and the annual influx of skiers who will test their edges on the mountain's smooth slopes.

Madonna Peak (foreground), at the Smuggler's Notch ski area south of Jeffersonville, pales in comparison to the grandiose Mount Mansfield (background).

The brilliant colors of fall seem to have ignited these hillsides outside Morrisville.

Nestled along the shores of Lake Memphremagog, Newport is the last large town you'll encounter in northeastern Vermont before entering Canada. The area is known as a sportsman's paradise for its wealth of fishing and hunting opportunities.

The Northeast Kingdom

Vermont's most rural region is its far northeast corner, which was aptly named the Northeast Kingdom by former U.S. Senator George D. Aiken roughly four decades ago. The name stuck because of the region's rural beauty and fiercely independent traditions. The villages here are less developed, less affluent, and farther apart than those of the Champlain and Connecticut Valleys, but residents of the Northeast Kingdom are proud of their homeland's remoteness and wild beauty. The region's open farmland, unspoiled vistas, and close-knit villages and small cities have attracted a rich mix of writers and artists to supplement the farmers and tradesmen who have long made the Northeast Kingdom a working landscape. Two of Vermont's most charming cities, St. Johnsbury and Newport, are the cultural and economic hubs of the region, and dozens of sparkling lakes make the region a summertime haven for vacationers and Vermonters alike.

—T. S.

As the Ice Age glaciers moved south, they both carved out Lake Willoughby and formed Mount Pisgah (foreground).

Island Pond is a small village outpost in Vermont's remote Northeast Kingdom.

The relatively flat land between Newport and Derby Line lends itself to growing large crops of corn. This tractor worked long hours to bring in its harvest of silage before the weather took a turn for the worse.

This farm straddles the border between Vermont and Canada at Derby Line.

A north wind excites the waters of Island Pond in the town of the same name, foretelling changing weather.

Because of its near-vertical cliffs and deep glacial waters, Lake Willoughby is known as the Lake Lucerne of New England.

At the northern end of Lake Willoughby is a sandy beach that attracts summer crowds seeking to cool off.

In the St. Johnsbury area, hundreds of miles of trails and numerous frozen lakes provide the snowmobiler with the opportunity to play during the long winter months.

The snow-covered rooftops of St. Johnsbury reminded me of a miniature village that my family used to place under our Christmas tree.

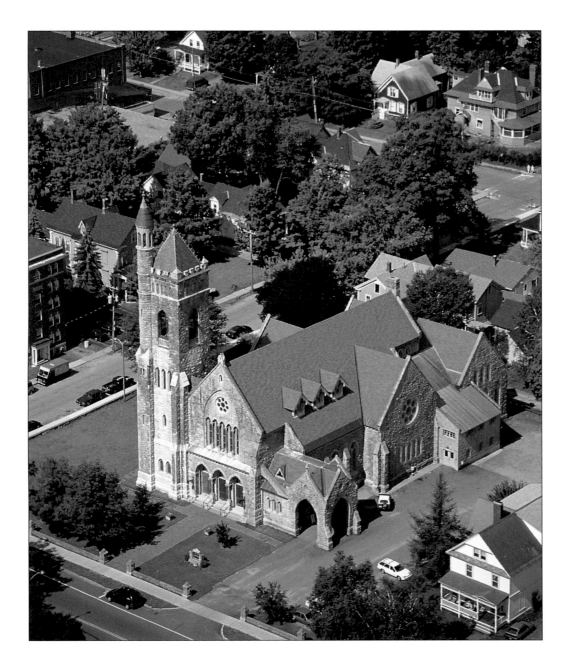

The builders of this church in St. Johnsbury made use of the plentiful stone in nearby quarries to preserve the structure's stoic image for centuries to come.

The late-afternoon sun casts long shadows from tall conifers onto a frozen lake in Groton State Forest, near West Danville.

A small aluminum boat awaits the disappearance of a summer's worth of algae growth on a small pond
in the hills near Danville.

This beautifully preserved round barn near Passumpsic is still being used. Hay is stored in its upper levels, while the ground floor provides shelter for livestock.

As I fly over the countryside, I am continually amazed at the lengths to which man will go to build a home with no apparent access, in the most remote of regions. Whoever put up this cabin, northwest of Barnet, cherishes his isolation and privacy.

The Connecticut River forms the eastern border between Vermont and New Hampshire. Rooty and I followed its meandering banks from Brattleboro to Barnet, flying above fertile farm fields and towns whose very existence depends on the water's energy.

The Connecticut River Valley

Just as the Champlain Valley dominates most of western Vermont, so the Connecticut River Valley is the defining region of eastern Vermont. From Brattleboro in the south to Ryegate and Barnet in the north, residents along much of the eastern slope of the Green Mountains look toward the river and think of themselves in relation to it. The Upper Valley is really a bi-state community defined more by the ecosystem of the river than by the political boundary that separates Vermont and New Hampshire. It is a refined and quietly civilized region of prosperous villages, like Norwich, and a settled lifestyle far removed from the erstwhile political power centers of Montpelier and Concord, New Hampshire.

Both Interstate 91, a modern superhighway, and U.S. Route 5, a quiet, winding two-lane road, parallel the river for much of its length alongside Vermont. They express the two sides of the present-day Connecticut River Valley, which has its hi-tech industries and contemporary concerns, but deeply values its traditions and strong sense of the past.

—T. S.

Cruising along west of Post Mills, I came upon the enchanting, snow-covered village of Strafford.

An old wooden covered bridge stands in stark contrast to a modern overpass on Interstate 91 as both span the Ottauquechee River, north of Hartland.

A large glass-roofed greenhouse along the banks of the Connecticut River near East Thetford presents an expansive array of abstract forms.

Flying over the Grafton area at sunset, high above the mountains, provided me and Rooty with
a truly mystical moment.

While the residents below were awakening to a gray, overcast sky, Rooty and I soared high above
the Connecticut River Valley near Fairlee, languishing in the calm air and observing Mother Nature
as she danced among the hills and valleys in her rippling garments of lacy fog and mist.

As the days of summer fade into crisp fall mornings, the valleys along the Connecticut River fill with convective fog. As the sun heats up the atmosphere and burns off the mist, it creates the illusion of a landscape in motion, as seen in this photograph, taken near Post Mills.

Spring colors burst forth in the Connecticut River valley, enhancing the beauty of the already picturesque village of Newbury.

Looking completely out of place in the hills of Vermont, the turquoise water of this sand mining pit near Perkinsville is more reminiscent of the Bahamas.

The White River and Interstate 89 slither around Billings Hill and the village of Sharon.

Known as "the cradle of inventions," Springfield is the home of such innovations as the common spring, clothespin, steam shovel, and corn planter.

The Black River surges through and around an old mill in Springfield. The city seems to have designed its streets and buildings in harmony with the river, rather than trying to tame the water's meandering course.

Rooty and I followed the Black River out of Springfield to its junction with the White River. Taking a hard left, we came upon this tranquil farm on the rich floodplain.

In the early part of the century, Bellows Falls was just one of many towns along the Connecticut River to harness the water's energy and use it in textile and paper manufacturing. Still clearly visible from above are the navigable canals, which were the first to be built in the nation. Today the water that runs through them is used to generate electric power.

The convergence of the White and Connecticut Rivers at White River Junction is marked by a plethora of cement and steel bridges.

The wooden structure that connects the banks of the Connecticut River between Windsor, Vermont, and Cornish, New Hampshire, is the longest two-span covered bridge in the world. It is the fourth to be built at this location, and tolls were collected here until 1943.

Colonel William Brattle, an early settler, is the source of the name of the modern city of Brattleboro. Nestled along the Connecticut River, it has become a year-round resort but continues to sustain considerable agricultural activity.